1DERBOY

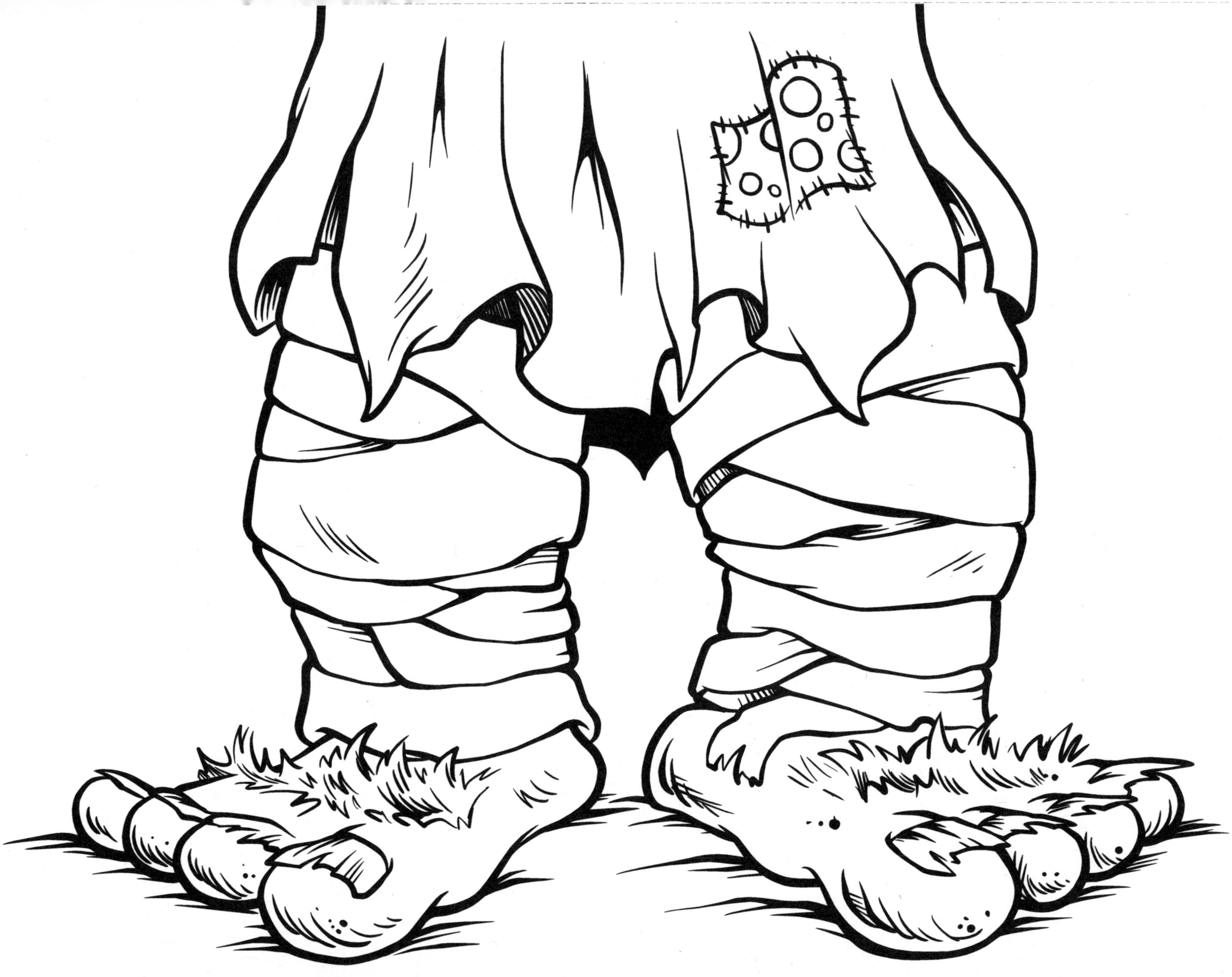

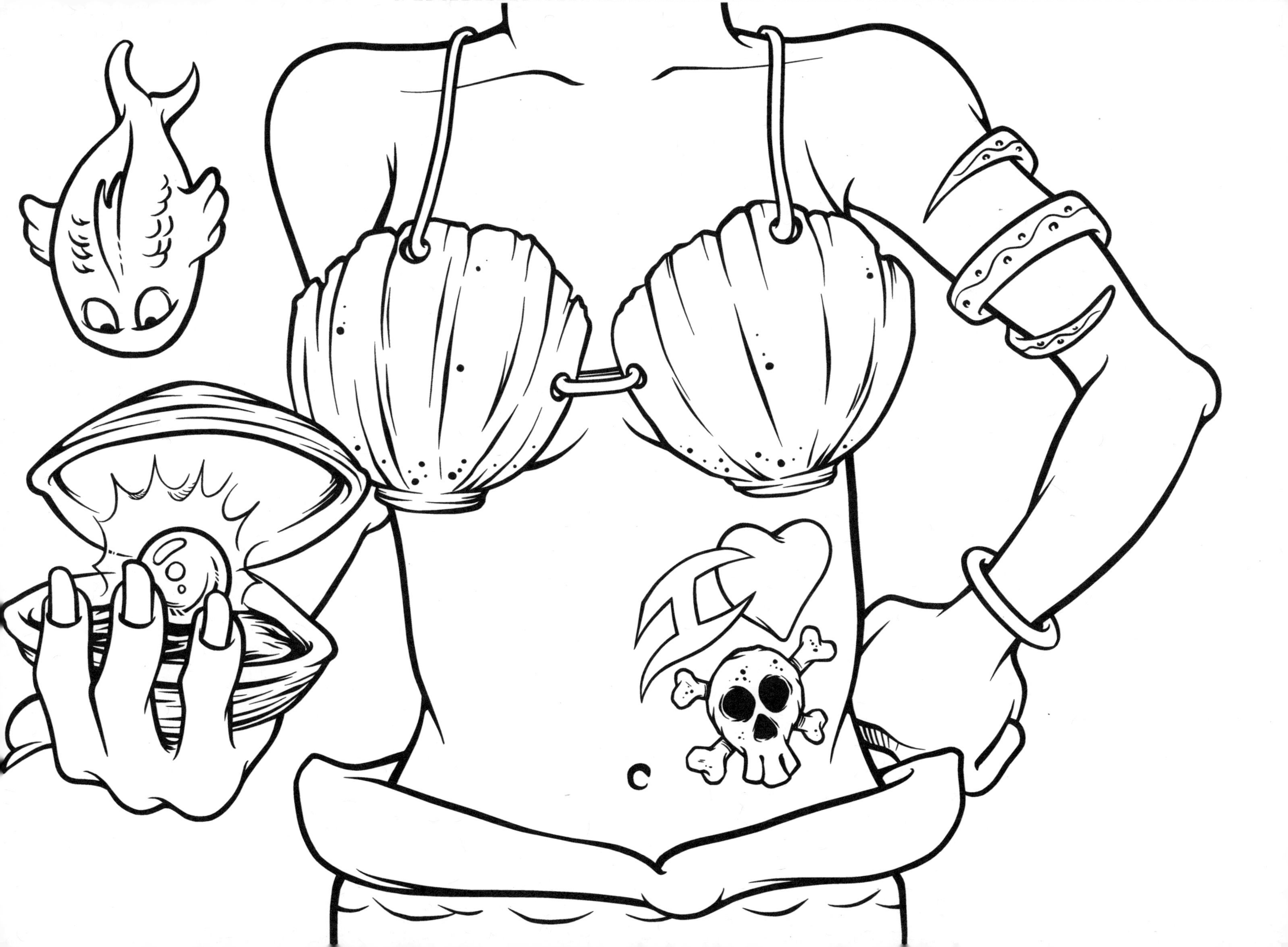

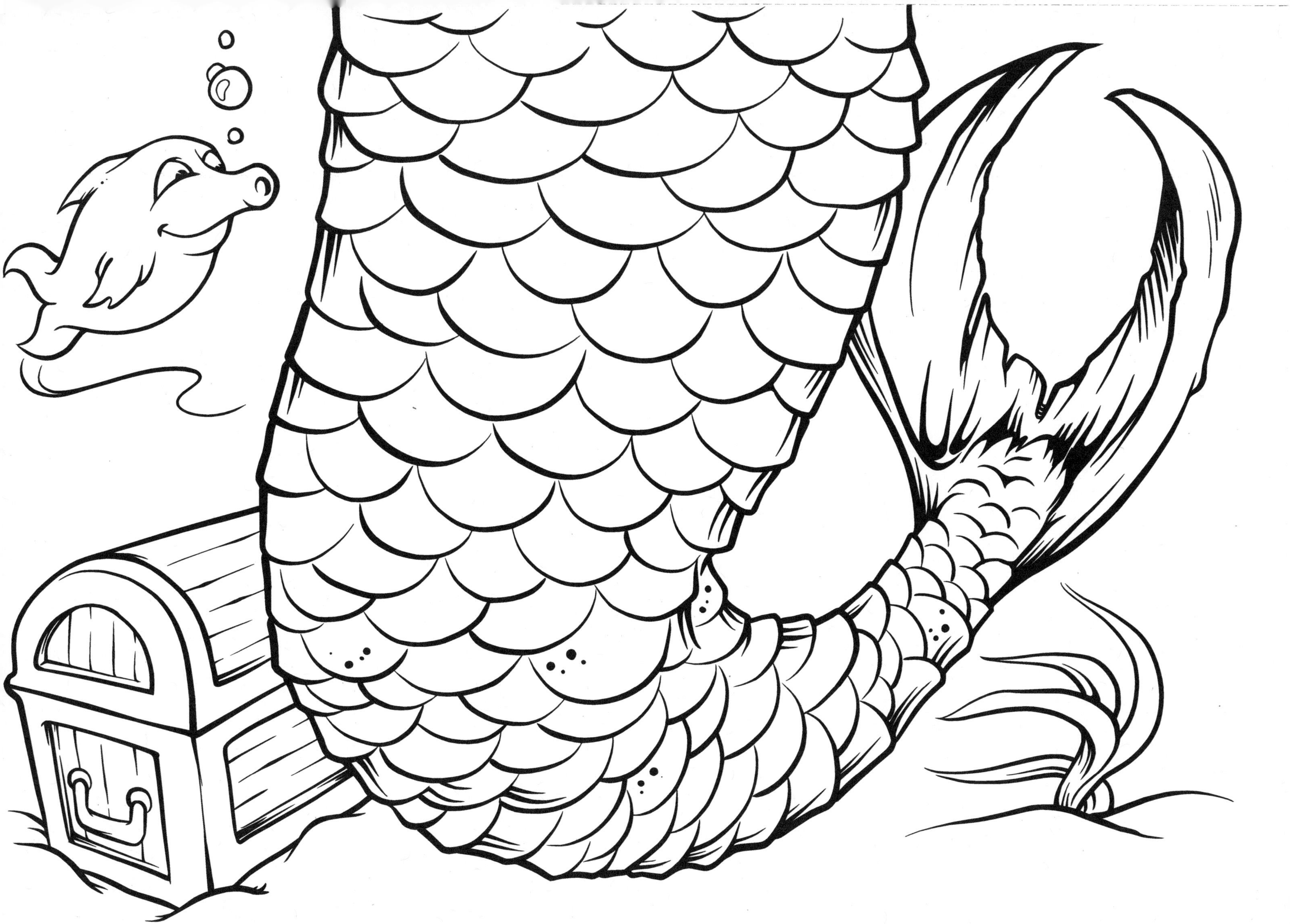

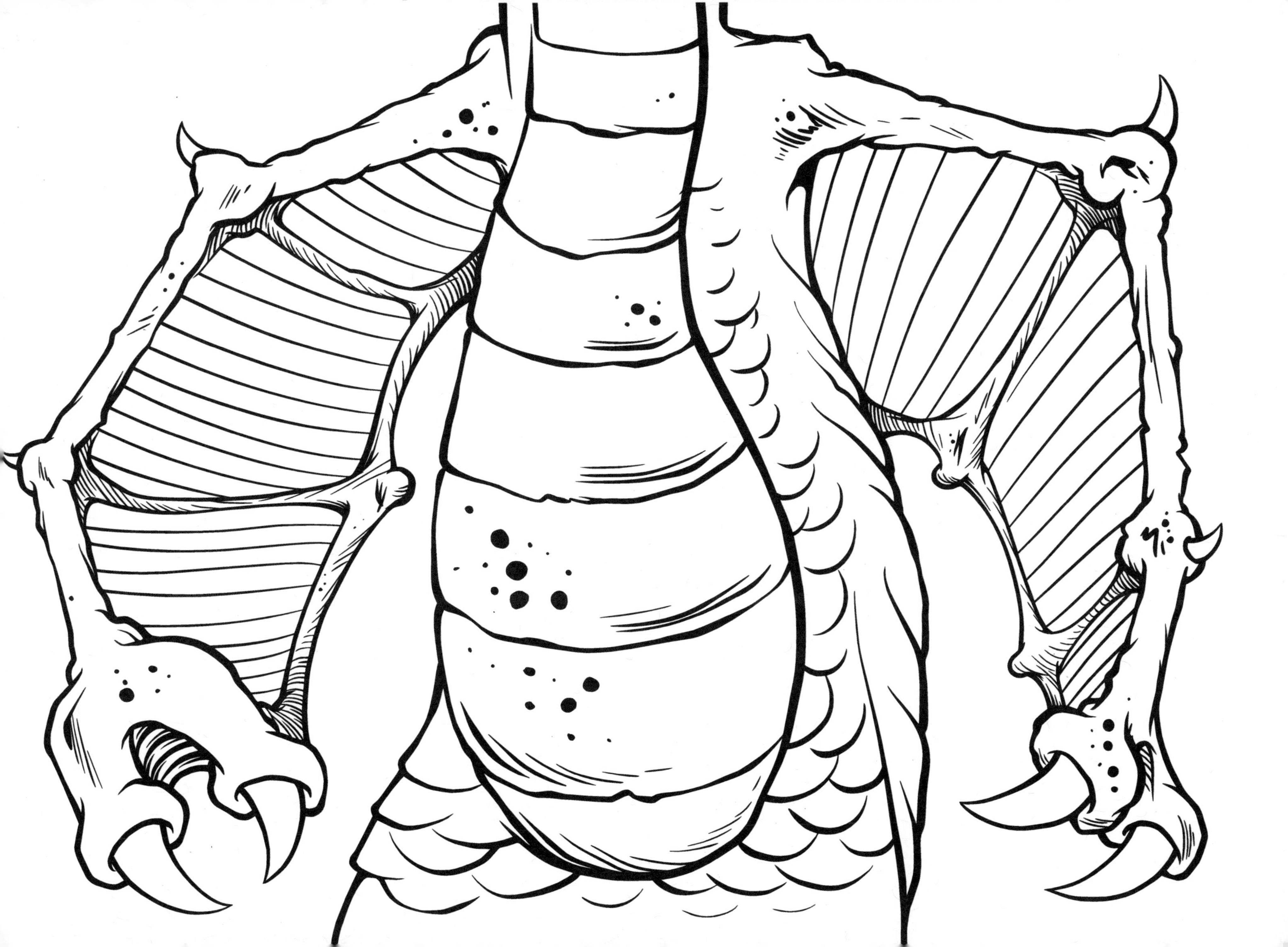

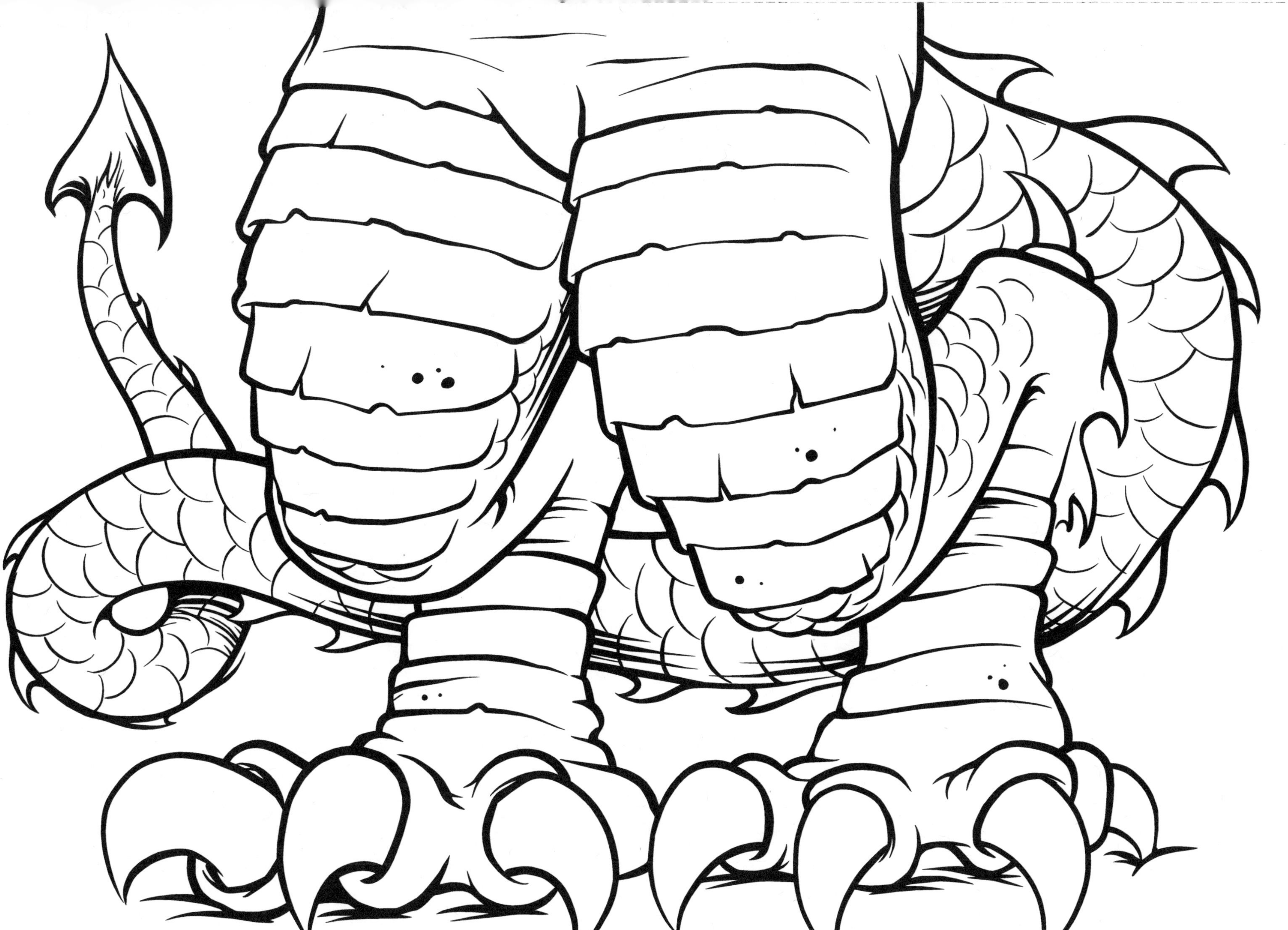

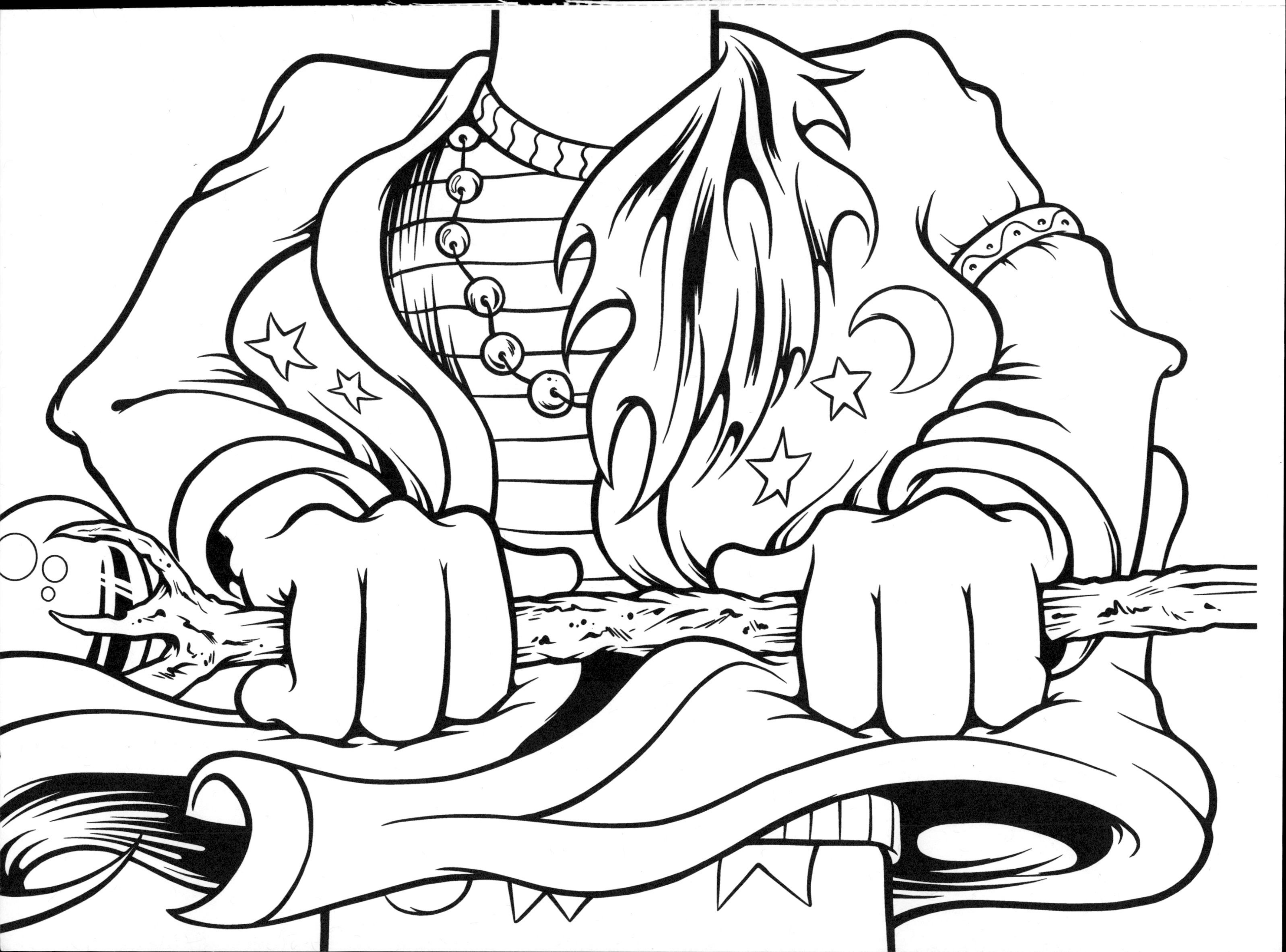

WizWear
WIZARD UNDERWEAR

TOOTH
Be Sold
BaBy Teeth

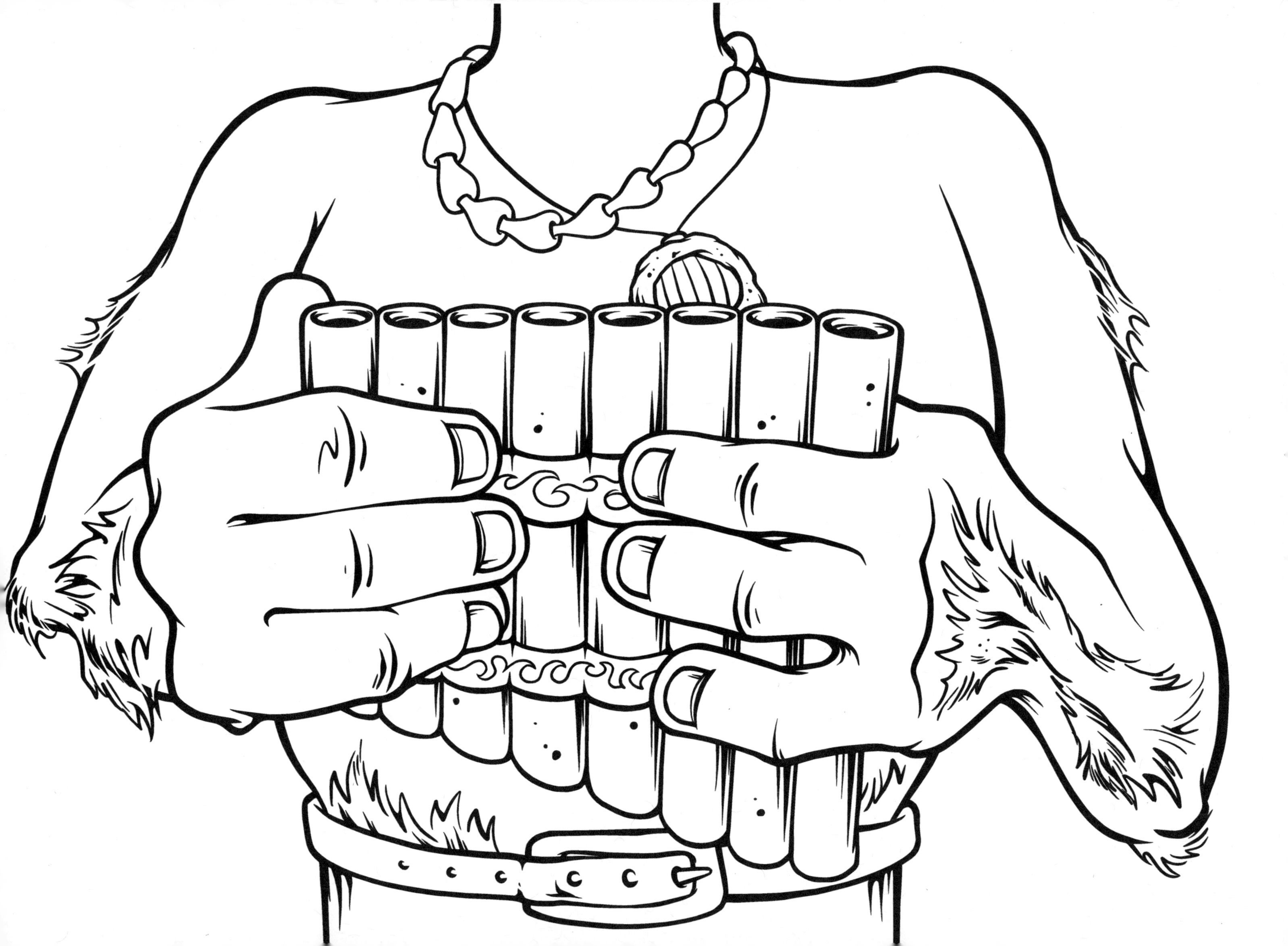

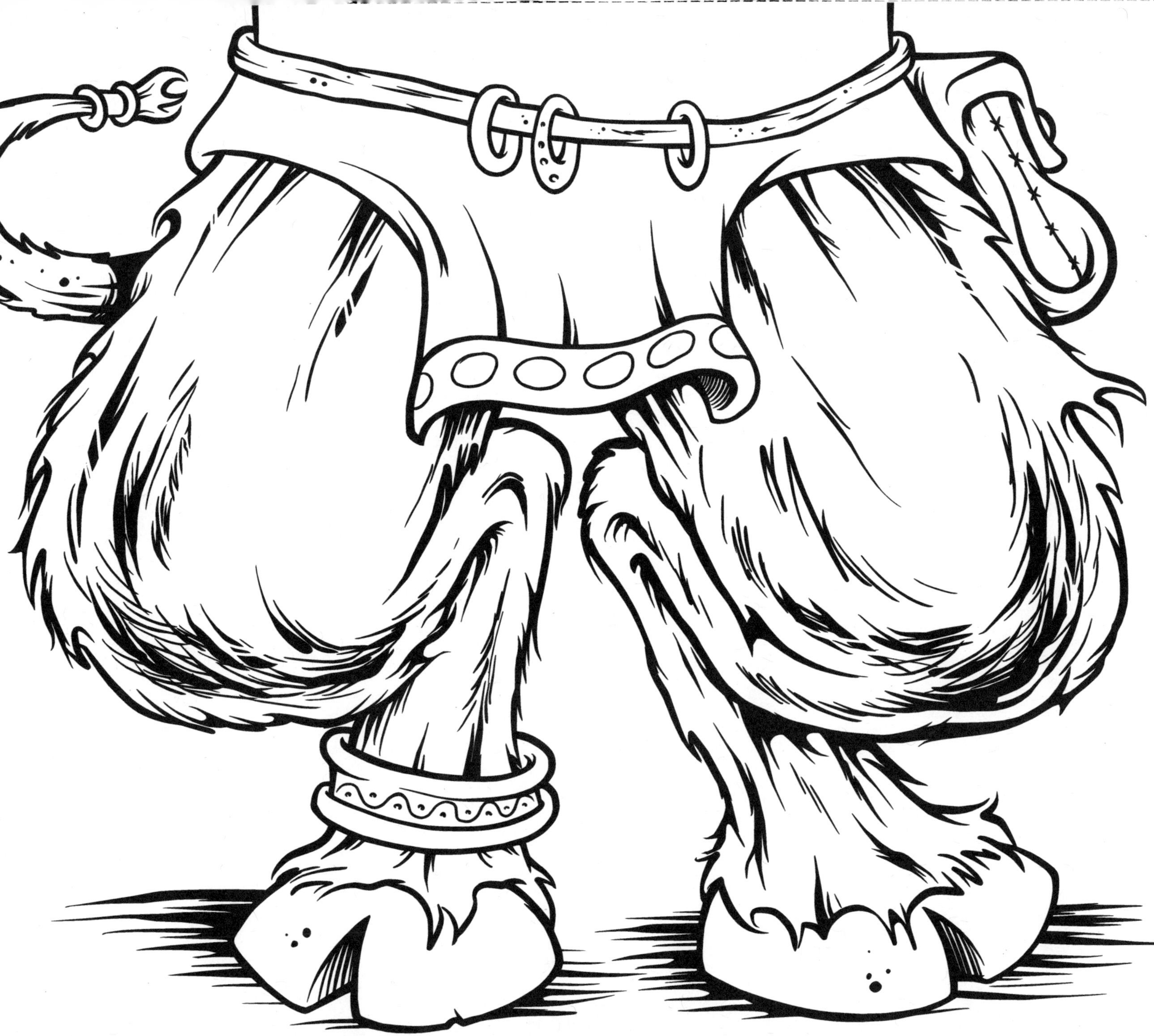

GOT
MOON

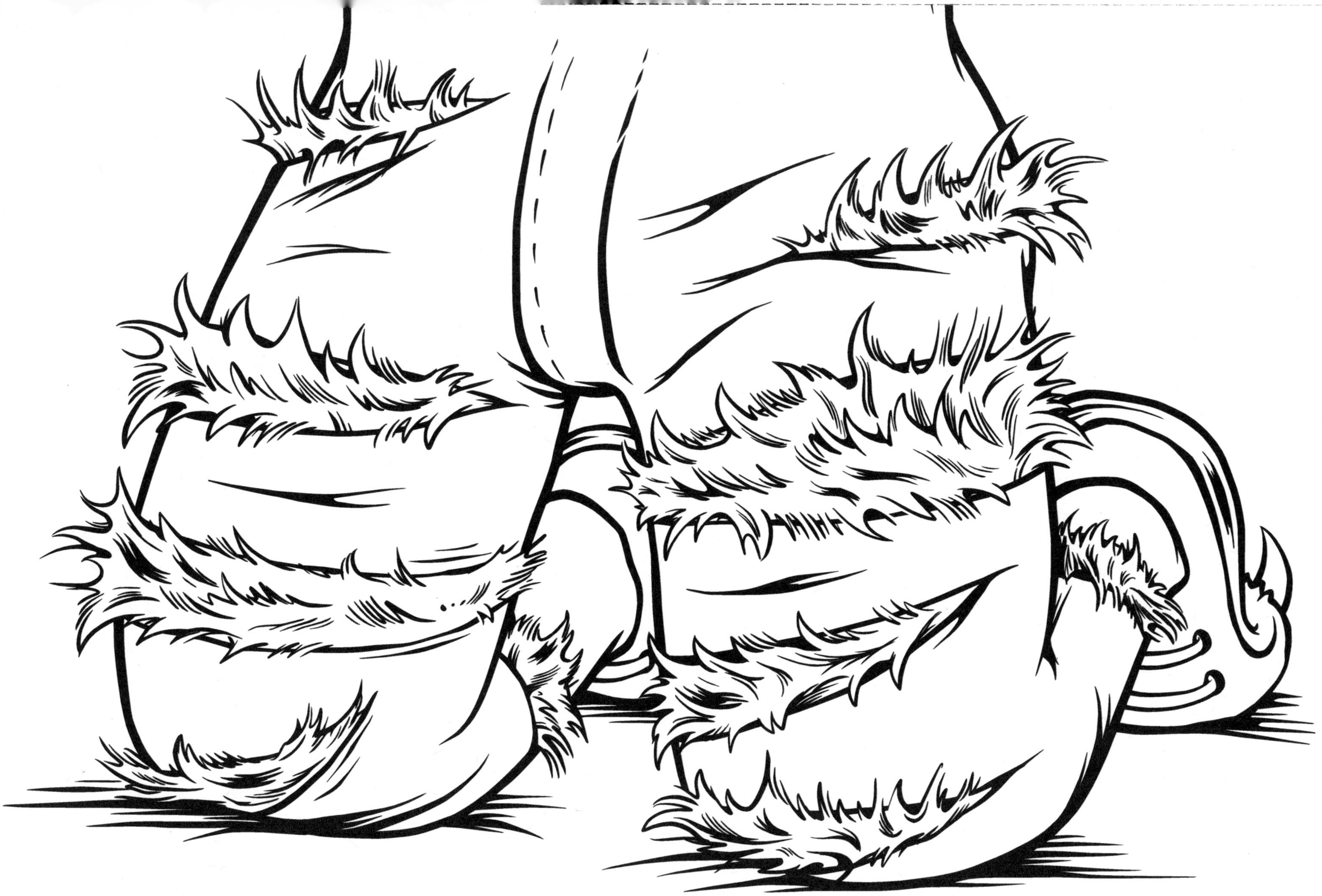